And now the word of the Lord
is ringing out from you
to people everywhere.

1 Thessalonians 1:8

bible belles

truth becomes her

Books may be purchased in quantity and/or special sales by contacting the publisher, Truth Becomes Her, at hello@biblebelles.com.

Published in San Diego by Truth Becomes Her. Truth Becomes Her and Bible Belles are registered trademarks.

This book was created as a result of hard work, prayers, coffee, prayers, a lot of late nights, prayers, so much help from others, prayers, and a whole bunch of God's grace. Did we mention prayers?

Illustrations by: Megan Crisp

Interior Design by: John Trent

Cover Design by: Ron Eddy

Editing by: Julie Monroe

Printed in the United States

ISBN: 978-1-7354611-2-0

The Adventures of Rooney Cruz

Ringleaders

A Devotional for Girls

written by
Erin Weidemann

illustrated by
Megan Crisp

CONTENTS

LETTER TO PARENTS

Welcome! I'm so glad you're here.

If you're reading this, it means you want to invest in a young woman you love. You want her to see herself the way God sees her—infinitely valuable, wondrously capable, and gracefully resilient.

Your girl has a powerful voice, but life, love, and leadership are about so much more than being loud. She has been called to deliver an important message: one that needs A Different Kind of Noise.

As a compliment to the Bible Belles Ringleaders Collection, these devotions will take you and your girl on a journey to discover how the stories of six extraordinary women worked together in perfect harmony to bring the good news of the gospel to the world for the very first time.

My hope is that your girl will be inspired by these stories to live her own life of love, faith, and fearlessness so she can carry forward God's message to her generation.

As you and your girl read through this devotional book, I pray you will have many meaningful moments with God and each other.

In your corner,
Erin Weidemann

Welcome, Ringleader.

Your adventure awaits . . .

ELIZABETH

DAY 1 AN IMPORTANT MESSAGE

1 Corinthians 14:8

Again, if the trumpet does not sound a clear call, who will get ready for battle?

Let's get right to it, shall we? A lot of girls struggle to be themselves. They have a hard time loving themselves as the unique and original people God created them to be. They don't really believe that their lives or their voices matter.

The truth is that God designed a life and plan for everyone, including you. He wants to guide you down a path to discover something really important: that your value lies in what God placed inside you and what He says about who you are.

God created you at this specific moment, in this exact place, for a very special purpose. He has a message He wants you to deliver, and He wants to team up with you to bring that message to the people in your home, neighborhood, community, and beyond.

Do you have to do it all by yourself? Of course not! God is going to help you every step of the way.

Isaiah 41:13

For I am the Lord your God who takes hold of your right hand and says to you, Do not fear; I will help you

God is going to show you how He really feels about you. He's going to show you how loved you are and how much He cherishes you. He is going to remind you that His plans for you are good and perfect and wonderful. And do you know what that's going to do? It's going to help you live in peace and confidence knowing that no matter what happens, God's love is always wrapped tightly around you.

DAY 2 *UPRIGHT IN GOD'S SIGHT*

In the Bible we can read about the women God chose to play a role in delivering His important message. God helped each one of them do the special job they were assigned to do. One of these women is Elizabeth. You can read about her in the gospel of Luke.

Read Luke 1:5–25.

The Bible calls Elizabeth "upright in the sight of God." She is praised for keeping all of God's commandments. A descendant of Moses' brother, Aaron, Elizabeth was chosen by God for a very specific purpose. She was to be the mother of John the Baptist, the greatest of all prophets.

God chose Elizabeth for the responsibility of raising and teaching John because she and her husband were faithful and honest, and because they respected and God and followed His instructions.

Activity: Discussion

Elizabeth's name means "God is my oath." *Oath* is another word for promise. Look up Psalm 84:11 and read it out loud. Then discuss the following questions.

1. *How is God a "sun and shield"?*

2. *The verse says, "The Lord gives grace and glory." What is the difference between grace and glory?*

3. *What are some other promises God made in the Bible?*

DAY 3 MIRACLE MAMA

When God chose Elizabeth to be the mother of John the Baptist, her life changed instantly. Elizabeth was older and had never had any children. At that time and in that culture, she would have felt extremely sad and embarrassed that she was not a mother.

But God changed all that. No longer was she known as a woman who couldn't have children; she became known as one who had a miraculous birth in old age.

Elizabeth was grateful that God met her in her sorrow and blessed her with a child. She was chosen to parent the one who would prepare the way for the Messiah. Elizabeth shows us that waiting on the Lord can bring unexpected blessings that are better and more wonderful than we ever could have imagined.

Mark 9:23

Everything is possible for the one who believes.

God wants to do miraculous things in your life too. When you experience sadness, doubt, or frustration about something you're going through, you can remember that God is not done working on the situation you're facing. Remain faithful to Him, following His ways and seeking Him in prayer and in His Word. You can prepare yourself so that you are ready for Him to move mightily!

Activity: Memory Verse

Job 5:9

He performs wonders that cannot be fathomed, miracles that cannot be counted.

DAY 4 STAY CONNECTED

Does the thought of God giving you an assignment make you feel nervous? Scared?

When God gives us an assignment, it's really important to stay close to Him as we carry it out. By praying and reading His Word daily, God can instruct us on how to approach doing the work He wants us to do.

John 15:5

"I am the vine; you are the branches. If you remain in me and I in you, you will bear much fruit; apart from me you can do nothing."

Challenge yourself today. Ask God to help you hear what He wants to tell you. Sit and listen for His still, soft voice. Jot down anything you feel like He's impressing on your heart. Remember, God is at work, and He wants you to stay connected to Him so He can work through you.

Activity: Drawing

Using today's verse from the gospel of John as inspiration, draw a picture of yourself as a long branch connected to and growing out from a strong, sturdy vine (God). Color it and hang it in your room as a reminder to stay connected to God.

DAY 5 A LIFE OF GRACE

What can we learn from Elizabeth's life of faith? First, Elizabeth believed in God's goodness and faithfulness. He made her a mother when many would have said it couldn't happen. Her story shows us that we can trust in God to fulfill His plan even when things seem absolutely impossible.

Elizabeth's son, John, was set apart by God for a special assignment. His job was to encourage the people to let go of a life of sin and turn to God.

Read John 1:57–60.

The name John means "The Lord is gracious." To be gracious is to be merciful, compassionate, kind, and forgiving. Doesn't that describe God's heart toward all of us? He chose John to prepare the people to receive His grace.

Titus 2:11–12

For the grace of God has appeared that offers salvation to all people. It teaches us to say "No" to ungodliness and worldly passions, and to live self-controlled, upright and godly lives in this present age.

What do these verses make you think about?
Write down your thoughts on the lines below.

DAY 6

A SONG OF SALVATION

Elizabeth's faith was steadfast, but her husband, Zechariah, learned the hard way to trust that what God says will come to pass. He lost his ability to speak when he challenged the angel in the temple about whether or not God could give him and Elizabeth a son. We read in Luke 1:61–66 that as soon as Zechariah confirmed what Elizabeth had said about the baby's chosen name, his speech was restored. And then, boy, did he have a lot to say!

Read Zechariah's Song in Luke 1:67–79.

When Zechariah could speak again, his first words were in praise to God. He spoke about the coming Savior God would use to save His people, and their son, John, was chosen to lead the way.

Activity: Discussion

Read verses 76–79 of Luke chapter 1 a second time. Then answer the following questions.

1. *Who is the "child"(v. 76) and how is God going to work through this child's life (v. 77)?*

2. *Who will "give light to those who sit in darkness" (v. 79)? How will He do it?*

DAY 7

PREPARE TO SHARE

Think about the last time you had to do something important. Whether it was a taking a test, competing in a tournament with your sports team, or playing your instrument at a music recital, preparation was an important part of the process.

Just like God designed a role specifically for Elizabeth, God has a special mission for you. And whenever we're on a mission with God, it's important to prepare.

Proverbs 24:27

Prepare your work outside
And make it ready for yourself in the field;
Afterwards, then, build your house.

Before you set out to accomplish a goal that lies in front of you, you must make proper preparations. Some people might want to skip ahead to the building without first preparing the field, but you won't make that mistake. You know God has an important message He wants you to share with the world, so you're going to get ready. Memorizing scripture so

God's Word is in your heart, spending time with Jesus so you really know how He is, and being kind and honest so people can trust you are all great ways to prepare.

Talk to your mom, dad, or another adult you trust. What are some things you can do now so you'll be ready when God calls you?

Activity: Prayer

Dear God,
I'm excited to find out more about the special message You have for me to deliver. What can I do now to get ready for this future challenge? Please show me any distractions or obstacles that are in my way right now. I want to know what they are and how I can remove them. Help me see more clearly what You want me to do to prepare myself for this assignment.
Amen.

NOTES

MARY

DAY 8

HIS GOOD PURPOSE

Did you know you have a unique and important part to play in God's story? The life He designed for you will be an ongoing adventure, one with many twists and turns along the way. Too often, though, we play it safe, thinking God's plans for us are small and insignificant. We assume that we are minor characters instead of major players.

Philippians 2:13

For it is God who works in you to will and to act in order to fulfill his good purpose.

God wants you to embrace the role you were born to play. He has a whole lot for each of His children to do during the course of their lives, and that includes you. You don't have to do any of the work in your own strength, though. God is going to work in and through you to accomplish His plans.

Spend a little time today talking to God about the plans He has for you. Ask Him about what He wants to do in you so that He can work through you. Use the lines below to write down what you believe He is telling you.

DAY 9 A CHANGE OF PLANS

Another young woman who didn't expect to be used by God in such a big way was Mary. Read about what happened in Luke 1:2–36.

God chose Mary for what some might say was the most important job in history—being the mother of God's Son, Jesus. Can you imagine? Mary was a young girl when the angel of the Lord came to her. Seriously, how did she not scream or run away when the angel visited her? How do you think you would have felt?

One thing's for sure, Mary did not expect that angel to show up. She had her own plans until God let her know that His plan was going to be very different from what she had imagined.

Think about a time when you experienced a change in plans. What happened? How did it make you feel? What do you believe God was showing you during that time?

DAY 10
THE ANSWER IS YES

Mary was a young girl just like you when God chose her for this assignment! She was an ordinary girl and then suddenly she found herself in the presence of the angel. She never could have expected to hear the most incredible news—that she would have a child, and her son would be the Messiah.

Read Luke 1:38.

Although Mary couldn't really understand how everything was going to happen, she responded to God by choosing to be faithful and obedient. She didn't worry about the details. She just said, "Yes."

Activity: Prayer

Dear God,

Please help me remember that You don't just give people jobs to do all on their own. You equip the people You choose for each and every task. You are faithful and good, and I know You will walk with me as I complete the work You have for me to accomplish. Please help me not to overthink or worry. Help me to simply respond with a yes, just like Mary did. No matter what happens, please help me say, "I am the Lord's servant. May your word to me be fulfilled."

DAY 11

GOING TOGETHER

Right after Mary received the news from the angel, she hurried to her cousin Elizabeth's house. When she arrived at Elizabeth's door, Mary called out to her. And as soon as Elizabeth heard Mary's greeting, she got quite a surprise. She felt the baby inside her belly jump!

Luke 1:41–45

When Elizabeth heard Mary's greeting, the baby leaped in her womb, and Elizabeth was filled with the Holy Spirit. In a loud voice she exclaimed: "Blessed are you among women, and blessed is the child you will bear! But why am I so favored, that the mother of my Lord should come to me? As soon as the sound of your greeting reached my ears, the baby in my womb leaped for joy. Blessed is she who has believed that the Lord would fulfill his promises to her!"

Elizabeth noticed something really important about Mary's faith. While Elizabeth's husband, Zechariah, had doubted what the angel told him about John, Mary trusted God and left right away to visit the one person who God prepared to help her —her cousin, Elizabeth!

Who are the people in your life who will help you in your journey to share God's special message? Make a list of people you can trust to encourage you along the way. Say a special prayer, thanking God for each of them.

DAY 12

LISTEN AND DO

Is it hard for you to do what you're told? When someone in charge tells you to do something, do you huff and puff? Do you whine or complain? Roll your eyes?

Most people don't like being told what to do or how to do something. They want to be independent and make their own choices. Have you ever thought about why? It's because we tend to think that we know best.

James 1:22

Do not merely listen to the word, and so deceive yourselves. Do what it says.

Often we don't really have any idea what the real best choice is. That's how we end up making mistakes. Sometimes, the mistakes are small. Sometimes they are bigger and cause ourselves and others a lot of problems.

But that is exactly why God gives us the truth. He's told us what He wants us to do, and He wants us to follow what His Word says. He wants us to obey.

Activity: Memory Verse

Deuteronomy 5:33

Walk in obedience to all that the LORD your God has commanded you, so that you may live and prosper and prolong your days in the land that you will possess.

DAY 13

FOR THIS IS RIGHT

Do you know one of the best ways to obey God? It's to obey your parents.

Ephesians 6:1–3

Children, obey your parents in the Lord, for this is right. "Honor your father and mother"—which is the first commandment with a promise—"so that it may go well with you and that you may enjoy long life on the earth."

Activity: Discussion

Read verses 1–3 from Ephesians 6 a second time. Then answer the following questions.

1. *Why do you think God cares if you obey your parents?*
2. *Why will your life be better if you obey your parents?*

Remember, the goal of obedience is not to make your parents happy. It is to please God and to practice so you can get good at obeying Him!

DAY 14

WALK IN LOVE

Obedience isn't as complicated as we make it out to be. When you choose to obey God, you are showing that you love Him.

2 John 1:6

And this is love, that we walk according to His commandments. This is the commandment, just as you have heard from the beginning, that you should walk in it.

A person who loves God makes a commitment to constantly work toward obedience. Someone who really loves Jesus will be constantly striving toward obedience, not thinking about how to bend the rules or get as close to the line as possible without going over.

You have a really cool opportunity in front of you. You get to show God how much you love Him by listening and doing what He says!

Activity: Drawing

Using today's verse from 2 John as inspiration, draw a picture of a path that God has laid out in front of you that represents His Word and instructions for how to live and obey Him. Color and hang it in your room as a reminder of how you get to show God that you love Him through your obedience.

NOTES

THE SAMARITAN WOMAN

DAY 15

LOVE AND LEAD

God has invited you to play an important role in His story. He loves you, and He created you to love Him back. One way you can do that is by following His teachings.

Another way you can love God is by talking about Him and His love with the people you know and meet. It's one of the ways He is calling you to be a leader.

1 John 4:19

We love because he first loved us.

Spend a little time today talking to God. Ask Him to show you some simple ways you can share about Him and show His love to others. What can you do and how can He help you? On the lines below, write down what you believe He is telling you.

DAY 16 LOVED OR LEFT OUT

Like Elizabeth and Mary, the Samaritan woman had an important role to play in God's story too. You can read about her in the gospel of John.

Read John 4:1–26.

Close your eyes and picture this woman for a minute. What do you think her life was like? She came to the well in the middle of the day when she expected no one would be there. Why was she alone? What burdens or struggles was she carrying?

The Samaritan woman was thirsty for more than just water that day. She was thirsty for something we all want. We all want to be loved. We all want to belong.

Think back to a time when you felt left out. How did you feel? What do you think would have helped you?

DAY 17

EVERY AND ALL

John 4:7

The Samaritan woman said to him, "You are a Jew and I am a Samaritan woman. How can you ask me for a drink?"

The Samaritan woman must have thought Jesus was out of His mind when He started talking to her. He was Jewish, and Jewish people didn't associate with Samaritans. Back then Jews and Samaritans had some bad feelings toward each other, so the fact that Jesus revealed who He was to a Samaritan woman is important. Jesus loves all people, no matter who they are or where they come from.

Even crazier, Jesus spoke to a woman. Jesus listened to her, answered her questions, and challenged her to consider her life. He didn't ridicule her or talk down to her. He engaged with a woman who was seen as an outcast in her culture. Jesus saw her for what she really was: God's creation, His beautiful child.

Activity: Memory Verse

John 1:12

Yet to all who did receive him, to those who believed in his name, he gave the right to become children of God.

DAY 18 SHOW AND TELL

How did the Samaritan woman respond when she realized Jesus was the Son of God?

John 4:28–30, 39

Then leaving her water jar, the woman went back to the town and said to the people, "Come, see a man who told me everything I ever did. Could this be the Christ?" They came out of the town and made their way toward him . . . Many of the Samaritans from the town believed in him because of the woman's testimony, "He told me everything I ever did."

The Samaritan woman's story teaches us a very important lesson. As soon as she met Jesus and found out who He really was, she knew she had to tell others about Him. She left her water jar and went back to her village. Some things are just too important not to share right away!

Psalm 105:1

Give praise to the Lord, proclaim his name; make known among the nations what he has done.

Activity: Drawing

Using today's psalm as inspiration draw a picture of you giving praise to the Lord and telling people about what He has done in your life. How has knowing about Jesus changed you? Color it and hang it in your room as a reminder to tell others about Him.

DAY 19 TO SEEK AND SAVE

Have you ever lost something really valuable? We all probably have at one time or another. Did you panic? Did you turn your room or your house upside down looking for it? That wonderful feeling of relief when we find our lost treasure is a hard one to top, isn't it? We draw in a deep breath and thank God we found what we had lost.

Luke 19:10

For the Son of Man came to seek and to save the lost.

Because of the Samaritan woman's boldness and bravery, other people in her town asked Jesus to stay with them. He stayed two more days, sharing His good news with them. As a result, many of the Samaritans came to believe in Him.

Jesus came to find what was lost. In this case, it was people. People who had fallen away from God or are separated from Him by sin. Jesus came to seek these people out and save them.

That is what Jesus wants us to do too. He wants us to be like the Samaritan woman, to go and find people who are lost and far away from God, share Jesus with them, and allow the Holy Spirit to bring them home!

Activity: Prayer

Dear God,
I want to show love to the people who are lost or far away from You. Please help me follow the Samaritan woman's example by telling people about Jesus.
Amen.

DAY 20 HIS PURPOSE FOR YOU

"God has a plan and you have a purpose."

Have you ever heard someone say something like that? There are a lot of people in the world wondering what their life's purpose is. Why were they born? Where are they meant to go and what are they meant to do?

Jesus knew exactly what His purpose was. He knew God sent Him into the world to seek and save the lost (Luke 19:10). He lived just how God called Him to live, and He didn't worry what other people thought about Him.

Just imagine for a second that you had that kind of confidence. One of the reasons Jesus' ministry was so powerful is that He taught with confidence. He knew who God made Him to be and He lived according to God's purpose for Him. And that is the challenge for all of us.

Activity: Discussion

God created you to follow Jesus and live like Him. One of your purposes is to point others to Jesus. Look up Matthew 9:37–38 and read it aloud. Then discuss the following questions.

1. *When Jesus said, "The harvest is plentiful but the workers are few"(v. 37), what did He mean?*

2. *Who are the "workers"(v. 38) that Jesus wants sent out into the harvest field? What does He want them to do?*

DAY 21 TELL IT LIKE IT IS

Has Jesus done something in your life that you could tell someone about? What was it? Using the lines below, describe what happened.

Whether we call it sharing our testimony, being a witness, or evangelism (fancy word alert!), Jesus has given us a simple command: tell others about Him. The more we practice, the easier it gets. Let's do it!

Activity: Memory Verse

1 Peter 3:15

But in your hearts revere Christ as Lord. Always be prepared to give an answer to everyone who asks you to give the reason for the hope that you have. But do this with gentleness and respect.

NOTES

MARY AND MARTHA

DAY 22

TIME WELL SPENT

Do you ever put unnecessary pressure on yourself to be and do more than God wants? Do you ever worry or fret over things that, in the big scheme of life, don't really matter so much?

One challenge we face in life is to stay focused on what God wants us to do without becoming distracted or sidetracked by less important things. We can do that by prioritizing things like obeying His teaching and sharing His love with others. We can also do it by spending time with Him.

1 Chronicles 16:11

Look to the LORD and his strength; seek his face always.

Spend a little time today thinking about the verse above. Seeking God's face is another way of seeking His presence. On the lines below, write down what you believe He wants you to know about spending time with Him.

DAY 23

WHAT IS BETTER

The story of Mary and Martha gives us some insight into how important it is to spend time with God. In the gospel of Luke, you can read about these two sisters and one of the many times Jesus visited their home.

Luke 10:38–42

Now as they went on their way, Jesus entered a village. And a woman named Martha welcomed him into her house. And she had a sister called Mary, who sat at the Lord's feet and listened to his teaching. But Martha was distracted with much serving. And she went up to him and said, "Lord, do you not care that my sister has left me to serve alone? Tell her then to help me." But the Lord answered her, "Martha, Martha, you are anxious and troubled about many things, but one thing is necessary. Mary has chosen the good portion, which will not be taken away from her."

Do you think Martha's heart was in the right place? Why or why not?

____

In verses 41–42, Jesus tells Martha there is only one thing that's really necessary for her to do. What is it?

Though many things in life can distract us, what does God want you to remember about spending time with Him?

DAY 24

PERFECT PEACE

As Jesus spent time in Mary and Martha's home, Mary sat at His feet. She listened intently to everything He was saying while Martha was busy tending to other things. It didn't take long for Martha to become angry and annoyed that her sister wasn't helping her.

When Martha asked Jesus to intervene, Jesus talked to her about choosing busyness and worry over simply resting in His presence and listening to Him.

Have you ever found yourself in a frenzy like Martha? What was causing you to worry so much?

Spend a little time with God today. Ask Him what He wants you to remember when you feel the urge to worry, stress, or fret about things (like Martha did)?

On the lines below, write down what you believe He is telling you.

Activity: Memory Verse

Isaiah 26:3

You will keep in perfect peace those whose minds are steadfast, because they trust in you.

DAY 25 READY TO RISE

This isn't the last time we read about Mary and Martha in the Bible. These two sisters and their brother, Lazarus, were some of Jesus' closest friends.

Read John 11:1–15.

When Lazarus was very sick, the sisters sent word to Jesus to come and heal him. But Jesus didn't come right away, and Lazarus died.

John 11:17–22

On his arrival, Jesus found that Lazarus had already been in the tomb for four days. Now Bethany was less than two miles from Jerusalem, and many Jews had come to Martha and Mary to comfort them in the loss of their brother.

When Martha heard that Jesus was coming, she went out to meet him, but Mary stayed at home.

"Lord," Martha said to Jesus, "if you had been here, my brother would not have died. But I know that even now God will give you whatever you ask."

Why do you think Jesus waited so long to come?

____

____

____

____

____

What did Jesus tell Martha in verse 23? Write it on the lines below.

____

____

____

____

____

DAY 26 RIGHT ON TIME

When you read the verses from yesterday's devotional, did it confuse you? I mean, couldn't Jesus have left sooner and healed His friend?

Once Jesus finally arrived, He told Martha, "Your brother will rise again" (v. 23). Read in John 11 the rest of their conversation.

John 11:24–26

Martha answered, "I know he will rise again in the resurrection at the last day."

Jesus said to her, "I am the resurrection and the life. The one who believes in me will live, even though they die; and whoever lives by believing in me will never die. Do you believe this?"

By delaying His arrival, Jesus stretched Martha's faith. He had a plan to raise her brother from the dead, all in God's perfect timing.

How did Martha answer Jesus' question (v. 27)?

There is absolutely nothing Jesus can't do. How does that make you feel? Write your thoughts on the lines below.

DAY 27 DEEPLY MOVED

After Martha spoke with Jesus, she went back and talked to her sister. Mary got up and quickly went out to meet Him. Read about what happened in John 11:32–35.

In these verses, we see Mary's sadness over the death of Lazarus and Jesus' emotional response to her grief. We know Jesus had already planned to raise her brother from the dead.

What does it mean in verse 35 when it says Jesus wept?

____

____

____

____

Why do you believe He did that?

____

____

____

____

2 Corinthians 1:5

For just as we share abundantly in the sufferings of Christ, so also our comfort abounds through Christ.

Jesus not only sees our pain, He feels it. He understands it. Knowing this, how might you care for or talk to others when they are experiencing sadness, grief, or pain?

____

____

____

____

DAY 28

ALIVE AGAIN

Jesus told Mary and Martha that their brother, Lazarus, would rise again, but the sisters didn't understand. Jesus had a plan. He went with the sisters to their brother's tomb and told them to open it. You can read about it in John 11:38–44.

Now think of all the different miracles Jesus performed during His ministry. Of all of His miracles, this is one was probably the most surprising. He made a dead man alive again!

If Jesus can do that, think about how much He can do in your life and in the lives of others.

Read Ephesians 2:1–10 and answer the following questions.

What does it mean that God has made you "alive in Christ" (v. 5)?

____

____

____

____

Not only are you alive in Christ, you were created in Christ for what purpose (v. 10)?

____

____

____

____

Activity: Prayer

Dear God,
Thank You for creating me with a special purpose—to point others toward Jesus. Help me live to serve You in what I say and do. Help me speak, act, and behave in a way that shows people what Jesus is really like. Amen.

NOTES

MARY MAGDALENE

DAY 29

YOUR POWERFUL VOICE

Throughout history, women have played a powerful role in advancing God's mission and building His kingdom. You have an important part to play too.

Psalm 68:11

The Lord announces the word, and the women who proclaim it are a mighty throng.

This verse shows us that God does not expect His warrior women to keep their mouths shut. God goes with His army, past and present, and you are part of that army! And when He claims a victory, His warriors announce the good news.

Hannah sang a song of thanksgiving. Deborah sang of victory over Sisera. Mary raised her voice to tell of God's goodness and grace.

These women did not keep quiet. There are countless other examples in the Bible of God moving in the lives of women and they, His daughters, lifted their voices. They spoke up about it! God wants you to do the same.

Spend a little time today talking to God. Reflect on Psalm 68:11. Ask Him about the ways He wants you to use your voice to become part of the "mighty throng" of women who proclaim His Word. Use the lines below to write down what you believe He is telling you.

DAY 30

INSTRUMENT OF INFLUENCE

One woman who found her voice and blazed an important trail for generations of other women is Mary Magdalene. Her devotion to Jesus put her in the spotlight of God's story, and we can learn so much from her life and faith.

Some people have assumed Mary was a really bad person who made a ton of mistakes. While there isn't a lot of evidence to back that up, the most important thing to remember is that Mary Magdalene isn't defined by who she was before she met Jesus. The only thing that matters is who she became after meeting and believing in Him.

2 Corinthians 5:17

Therefore, if anyone is in Christ, the new creation has come: The old has gone, the new is here.

When we encounter Jesus, we can follow Mary's example. We shouldn't simply return to the life we left. He changes everything. Our whole life can be about following, serving, and sharing Him!

DAY 31 CHOOSING TO STAY

Mary Magdalene was a loving and faithful disciple of Jesus. She was one of the women who stayed with Jesus, even to His death on the cross.

Read Mark 15:33–41.

Mary Magdalene stayed near to Jesus even though many others abandoned him.

How did her presence show her love for Jesus?

____

____

____

____

Do you think it was difficult for her to stay with Him? Why or why not?

____

____

____

____

Mary Magdalene shows us that even though we experience struggles and sadness, we can continue serving God and trusting in Him. Do you agree? Why or why not?

DAY 32

SPEAKING UP

Mary wasn't just there at Jesus' death on the cross. She was there at the tomb and was the first person to see and talk with Jesus after His resurrection. Read about her encounter with Jesus in John 20:1–18.

What did Mary do immediately after Jesus appeared to her?

God wants you to use your voice just like Mary Magdalene did to share the gospel. Your voice has the power to comfort those who are suffering. It can encourage, love, inspire, and teach. There are so many different ways to use it!

Activity: Prayer

Dear God,

Thank You for the opportunity to share Your love with others. Please help me use my voice with wisdom and bravery. I don't want to just add to the noise. Please show me how I can use my voice to help people come to know and follow Jesus. Help me be brave in sharing Jesus with people wherever you take me in my life.

Amen.

DAY 33

THE MINISTRY OF MEETING NEEDS

We know Mary Magdalene was the first person to see Jesus alive after His death. What else do we know about her?

Mary Magdalene, along with other women, followed and ministered with Jesus as He traveled and taught in Galilee. You can read about these women in Luke 8:1–3.

The women who accompanied Jesus had been healed by Him, and they helped support Jesus and His followers "out of their own means." This means the women contributed money that provided for the needs of the group. These women weren't just following the men around. They were active participants in proclaiming the gospel and God's kingdom. They weren't sitting on the sidelines warming the bench. They were major league players!

Activity: Discussion

Read Luke 8:1–3 a second time. Then discuss the following questions.

1. *What does it mean to you to know that women played such an important role in helping Jesus carry out His earthly ministry and mission?*

2. *What are some ways you can share Jesus with people "out of your own means"?*

DAY 34

SHARING THE WORK AND REWARD

Now that you know more about Mary Magdalene and the women who accompanied Jesus and His other disciples, maybe you're wondering something.

Why didn't Jesus miraculously provide for His ministry and its followers? He did countless other miracles. Couldn't He have done the same to meet the daily needs of His group?

I think it's because Jesus wanted these women to be a vital part of His team. Throughout Jesus' life and ministry, He loved, respected, and included women. His disciples were men and women. He gave both men and women the opportunity and privilege of being part of His mission.

Those who share in the costs of ministry get to participate as partners in that ministry. What a blessing! These women sustained Jesus in His work and they get to share in the reward!

Activity: Memory Verse

Matthew 12:49–50

Pointing to his disciples, he said, "Here are my mother and my brothers. For whoever does the will of my Father in heaven is my brother and sister and mother."

DAY 35

TRAINED AND SENT

Mary Magdalene was the first to see the empty tomb and to hear the truth about Jesus' resurrection. She fulfilled Jesus' command by going to tell the disciples what had happened. By announcing the good news of Jesus' resurrection, Mary Magdalene was transformed from one of Jesus' disciples to an apostle.

Do you know the difference between a disciple and an apostle?

A disciple is someone who is *trained by a teacher.*

An apostle is a messenger, "a person sent forth with orders." An apostle is *sent out to represent the teacher.*

Activity: Drawing

Fold a piece of drawing paper in half. On the left side, draw a picture of you sitting at Jesus' feet, learning from Him. On the right, draw yourself as a representative of Jesus, going out to share the gospel with others. Color it and hang it in your room as a reminder to be both a disciple and apostle of Jesus.

NOTES

The Leading Role

DAY 36

WHEN WE CARE, WE SHARE

When you really care about something, do you keep it to yourself?

When something is meaningful or important to us, we share it. We want others to enjoy it too!

Ringleader, this is your moment. You've reached an important step in your life and leadership.

There are people in the world who know about Jesus but have chosen not to follow Him. There are also people who don't know about Jesus and have never even heard His name. They don't know that Jesus is God's Son, that He loves them, or that He died to save them.

God's message for you is the same one He wants you to deliver to others. It's the gospel—the good news of Jesus. You have been given an important role in God's story: to deliver the message of Jesus' life, death, and resurrection and to invite others to believe and trust in Him.

Romans 10:14

How, then, can they call on the one they have not believed in? And how can they believe in the one of whom they have not heard?

What does this verse mean to you? Write your thoughts on the lines below.

____

____

____

____

____

DAY 37 *YOUR LIFE MATTERS*

"I really want my life to matter, to mean something. All of these women—Elizabeth, Mary, the Samaritan woman, Mary and Martha, Mary Magdalene—they all played an important role in Your story. Now I know I can too."

God has an important part for you to play in sharing Jesus with others just as He did for Rooney. He wants you to share about Him through your words and actions.

Colossians 3:17

And whatever you do, whether in word or deed, do it all in the name of the Lord Jesus, giving thanks to God the Father through him.

Activity: Prayer

Dear God,
I realize it's not about me. It's about Jesus. I can shine the spotlight on Him, no matter where I go or what I do. There are people everywhere who need to know about You. Show me how I can help deliver this important message to others.

DAY 38

THE RINGLEADER'S MISSION

Look up and read Matthew 18:16–20. This command Jesus gave to His disciples is known as the Great Commission. In it Jesus tells His disciples to take the gospel to every person throughout the world and to make disciples in all nations.

If we are followers of Jesus, we need to take this command seriously. That means we must dedicate ourselves to fulfilling it out of love and gratitude for what Jesus has done for us. That's what being a Ringleader is all about!

Activity: Memory Verse

Acts 20:24

However, I consider my life worth nothing to me; my only aim is to finish the race and complete the task the Lord Jesus has given me—the task of testifying to the good news of God's grace.

DAY 39

A WILLING WITNESS

When you hear the word *witness,* what comes to mind? Do you imagine someone sitting in a courtroom explaining to the judge what they saw?

After He was raised from the dead, Jesus told His apostles they should be faithful witnesses. He told them the Holy Spirit would give them power to spread the word about God's kingdom.

"You will be my witnesses," He told them, "in Jerusalem, throughout Judea and Samaria, and to the ends of the earth" (Acts 1:8).

Remember, witnessing isn't just something we do. It's who we are.

1 Thessalonians 1:8

And now the word of the Lord is ringing out from you to people everywhere.

Activity: Drawing

Using today's verse from 1 Thessalonians as inspiration draw a picture of the good news "ringing out from you to people everywhere." You sharing Jesus with others through your life, words, and actions. Color it and hang it in your room as a reminder that you are His witness.

DAY 40 WHAT MATTERS MOST

Have you ever wondered what matters most to God? Of everything He created, what does God treasure most?

It's people. It's you!

God loves His children, each and every one. He wants to spend eternity with them in heaven.

Ringleader, you have been given the opportunity to draw others close to Him so they can experience His love and salvation through Jesus. Make the most of it!

John 15:8

"This is to my Father's glory, that you bear much fruit, showing yourselves to be my disciples."

Since you began this journey, how has your faith grown?

Now that you know more about being a Ringleader, what do you want to do differently?

What do you believe God is telling you right now?

NOTES